September 11, 2001

September 11, 2001

Dennis Brindell Fradin

Marshall Cavendish
Benchmark

New York

Marshall Cavendish Benchmark
99 White Plains Road
Tarrytown, NY 10591
www.marshallcavendish.us

Library of Congress Cataloging-in-Publication Data

Fradin, Dennis B.
September 11, 2001 / by Dennis Brindell Fradin.
p. cm. — (Turning points in U.S. history)
Includes bibliographical references and index.
Summary: "Covers the 9/11 terrorist attacks as a watershed event in U.S. history, influencing social, economic,
and political policies that shaped the nation's future"—Provided by publisher.
ISBN 978-0-7614-4259-2
1. September 11 Terrorist Attacks, 2001—Influence—Juvenile literature. 2. War on Terrorism, 2001—-Juvenile literature. 3. United States—
Politics and government—2001—-Juvenile literature. 4. United States—Social conditions—21st century—Juvenile literature. I. Title.
HV6432.7.F734 2010
973.931—dc22
2008038267

Photo Research by Connie Gardner
Cover photo by Chris Hondros/Getty Images
Cover: The wreckage of the World Trade Center, September 13, 2001
Title Page: Twin beams of light rise near Ground Zero, September 11, 2003.

The photographs in this book are used by permission and through the courtesy of: *Associated Press:* John Marshall Mantel, 3; AP Photo, 20;
Carmen Taylor, 22; Gary Tramontina, 31; Amel Emrie, 37; *Corbis:* Hubert Boesl, 6; Wyman Ira, 8; Barney Burstein, 10; Bettmann, 13; Reuters, 16, 23, 28;
Richard Cohen, 27; Catherine Leuthold, 32; *Getty Images:* AFP, 14; Time and Life, 17; Spencer Platt, 24; Joe Raedie, 35; *The Image Works:* Romel Pecson, 39.
Timeline: *Corbis:* Hubert Boesl.

Editor: Deborah Grahame
Publisher: Michelle Bisson
Art Director: Anahid Hamparian
Printed in Malaysia
1 3 5 6 4 2

Contents

Lower Manhattan fills with smoke and debris on the morning of September 11, 2001.

CHAPTER ONE

What Was 9/11?

On September 11, 2001, **terrorists** attacked the United States. Nineteen terrorists in four groups **hijacked**—took control of—four flying jet planes. They crashed two of the jets into New York City's two tallest buildings. They crashed a third jet into an important government building outside Washington, D.C. A fourth jet crashed into a field after passengers fought with the hijackers.

About three thousand people died in these terrorist attacks. Most were in the buildings that the hijacked jets hit. Hundreds more were passengers and crew members aboard the four planes. All nineteen hijackers also died when the four jets crashed.

American Airlines personnel and others gather on September 12, 2001, to pray and grieve outside Boston Town Hall.

People often write dates using numbers. For example, the Fourth of July is written 7/4 because it is the fourth day of the seventh month. September 11 is written 9/11—the eleventh day of the ninth month. The events of

What Is Terrorism?

Terrorism involves violent acts carried out by people who are not an official army against a group they consider their enemy. Terrorists often kill people. Sometimes they take **hostages** and threaten to kill them if the terrorists' demands are not met. Terrorists plan their acts in secret and usually strike suddenly and unexpectedly. Part of their goal is to terrorize, or scare, an entire nation or group.

September 11, 2001, became known as the 9/11 terrorist attacks. Many people refer to the event simply as 9/11.

The events of 9/11 not only saddened and enraged Americans. They also raised difficult questions. How could anyone be cruel enough to kill thousands of people they did not even know? What would the United States do to strike back at **terrorism**? How could future attacks be **prevented**?

Ancient Persia was the setting for this fifteenth-century painting of two Mongol warriors.

CHAPTER TWO

Centuries of Conflict

Humans have fought each other throughout history. They have fought over boundaries between countries. They have fought over differences in skin color, religion, and many other things.

Members of three major religions have been in conflict many times. One is Judaism, the world's first religion to declare that there is a single God. The second is Christianity, the faith based on Jesus Christ's teachings. The third is Islam, founded by the religious teacher Muhammad.

For a long time, the three religions have fought over Palestine, also called the Holy Land. Palestine was where Judaism and Christianity began. It is also a **holy** place for Muslims, as believers of Islam are called.

Arab Muslims took control of Palestine in the 600s CE. From 1096 to 1270 CE, European Christians tried to take Palestine from the Muslims. They sent a series of **expeditions**, called Crusades, to try to **seize** the Holy Land. The Crusaders fought battles with the Muslims, but they failed to win permanent control of the Holy Land. The Crusades created bitter feelings between Christians and Muslims.

Terms of Confusion

Many people are confused by the terms *Islam*, *Muslims*, and *Arabs*. Islam is a religion, and the people who follow it are called Muslims. Arabs are people who originally come from Saudi Arabia, Iraq, and other countries of the Middle East, as well as northern Africa. Most Arabs are Muslims. However, some Arabs are Christians.

During World War II (1939–1945), Germans who belonged to the Nazi Party killed millions of Jewish people. After the war, in 1948, the nation of Israel was created for the remaining Jewish people. Israel includes much of Palestine. Hundreds of thousands of Arab Muslims were driven off the land to make way for Jewish settlers in the new country. This created bitter feelings between Jewish people and Muslims.

Israel has fought wars with its Muslim neighbors from time to time. In addition, Muslim terrorists have attacked Israelis. The terrorists have

Palestinian women and children cross into Arab territory after removal from their homes, June 1948.

bombed buses and markets in Israel. At the 1972 Summer Olympics, terrorists killed eleven Israeli athletes.

The United States is an **ally** of Israel. The U.S. armed forces have stationed troops in Muslim lands such as Saudi Arabia. For these reasons, Muslim terrorists began to target the United States, too.

This 1998 photo shows Osama bin Laden speaking somewhere in Afghanistan in front of a banner decorated with Arabic script.

CHAPTER THREE

Events Leading to 9/11

By the 1990s, a Saudi Arabian man named Osama bin Laden had become a terrorist leader. Bin Laden led a terrorist group called al-Qaeda, whose name means "the base" in Arabic. With bin Laden as its leader, al-Qaeda encouraged, trained, and gave money to Muslim terrorists. They attacked people they considered enemies of the Muslims. Osama bin Laden especially hated the United States. He called Americans "Crusaders." He encouraged his people to kill these enemies: "To kill the Americans and their allies—**civilians** and military—is an individual duty for every Muslim who can do it in any country in which it is possible to do it."

Osama bin Laden and al-Qaeda have been linked to several terrorist acts

An office worker in breathing distress is helped by police after the 1993 World Trade Center attack.

targeting the United States. In 1993 someone planted a bomb at one of the Twin Towers at New York City's World Trade Center. The explosion killed six people and injured a thousand more. However, it did not knock down the Twin Towers as the bombers had hoped. Some people believe that Osama bin Laden and al-Qaeda were behind this terrorist attack, but it was never proved.

The gash on the side of the USS *Cole* was caused by a suicide boat bomb in October 2000.

Five years later, in 1998, al-Qaeda bombed the U.S. **embassies** in the African countries of Kenya and Tanzania. Three hundred people died this time. On October 12, 2000, al-Qaeda terrorists bombed the USS *Cole*, an American ship that was refueling in the country of Yemen. Seventeen U.S. sailors died in the attack. By then, al-Qaeda was plotting a far bigger attack on the United States.

Osama bin Laden organized a group of al-Qaeda terrorists. Most of these men were from Saudi Arabia. All of them hated the United States. In fact, they were willing to die in order to kill a large number of Americans.

After coming to the United States, several of bin Laden's men learned how to fly airplanes by attending flying schools. The plan was for the terrorists to board four different passenger jets on the same morning. They would sneak weapons onto the planes. Once in the air, they would use the weapons to hijack the aircraft. They would then fly the airplanes straight into four important American buildings.

Two of the buildings were the Twin Towers of the World Trade Center. These were the same buildings that terrorists had tried to blow up in 1993. The Twin Towers were New York City's tallest buildings. Each tower was 110 stories tall—about 1,360 feet (415 meters) high. Many thousands of people worked in each tower.

The third airplane would fly into the Pentagon near Washington, D.C. This huge, five-sided building is home to the U.S. Department of Defense.

One of two Washington, D.C. buildings—the U.S. Capitol or the White House—was the fourth jet's target. The Capitol is the lawmaking center of the United States. The U.S. Senate and House of Representatives meet there. The White House is where the U.S. president and his family live.

The date that the terrorists chose to carry out their plan was Tuesday, September 11, 2001.

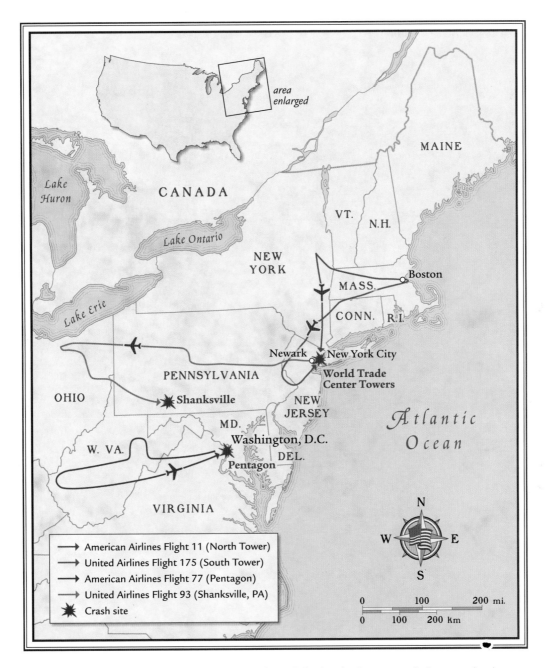

This map shows the routes of the four hijacked planes and the crash sites.

Two hijackers are shown on a surveillance video as they go through a security checkpoint before boarding American Airlines Flight 77.

CHAPTER FOUR

The 9/11 Hijackings

The terrorists bought their airline tickets between August 26 and September 5, 2001. They chose four flights that were scheduled to go cross-country from the East Coast to the West Coast. On this 2,500-mile (4,000-kilometer) trip, planes carried lots of jet fuel. If the planes hit buildings, there would probably be huge explosions and fires.

On the morning of 9/11, everything went as planned for the nineteen terrorists. They **smuggled** knives into the airport without anyone noticing. They boarded the four airplanes. They took their seats like the other passengers.

American Airlines Flight 11 departed from Boston at 7:59 AM. It was bound for Los Angeles. About fifteen minutes into the flight, five terrorists

A photographer captured the image of the jet airliner moments before it slammed into the south World Trade Center tower at 9:02 AM.

hijacked the airplane. They changed its course toward New York City. At 8:46 AM, Flight 11 crashed into the North Tower of the World Trade Center.

United Airlines Flight 175 took off from Boston at 8:14 AM. It, too, was bound for Los Angeles. A half hour into the flight, another five terrorists seized control of the aircraft. At 9:02 AM, they flew the plane into the South Tower of the World Trade Center.

At 8:20 AM, American Airlines Flight 77 departed from Washington, D.C. Flight 77 was also scheduled to fly to Los Angeles. However, a half hour into the flight, yet another five terrorists took

Outside the damaged Pentagon, firefighters join the rescue efforts.

over the aircraft. They turned the big passenger jet back toward the nation's capital and crashed it into the Pentagon.

At 8:42 AM, United Airlines Flight 93 took off from Newark, New Jersey, bound for San Francisco. About forty-five minutes into the flight, four terrorists hijacked the jetliner. They turned it toward Washington, D.C. However, their plan failed. Something unexpected would prevent them from crashing the aircraft into the U.S. Capitol or the White House.

Both north and south towers of the World Trade Center were engulfed in flames as a result of the jets' fuel explosions.

CHAPTER FIVE

"The Most Horrific Scene"

The airplanes that hit the Twin Towers were traveling at about 500 miles (800 km) per hour. Everyone aboard the two aircraft died as soon as the planes hit. At the time of the crashes, about 20,000 people were in the many business offices inside the Twin Towers. Hundreds of them were killed by the crashes. Explosions of jet fuel rocked the buildings. Fires broke out and spread.

Most people in the Twin Towers were able to get out safely. Firefighters and other emergency workers rushed to the scene and helped many of these people. Many others—especially people on upper floors—could not escape. As smoke and flames closed in on them, people made farewell calls to their loved ones.

One man phoned his wife, who was not home. Later she played the last message she would ever get from him. "I don't know if I'm going to get out, but I love you very much," he said.

Another man called his wife and told her, "I don't think I am going to make it. I love you. Take care of the children." He did not make it out alive, either.

The worst was yet to come. Weakened by the fires, the Twin Towers could no longer support themselves. The South Tower came crashing down at 9:59 AM. The North Tower fell at 10:28 AM. When they collapsed, the Twin Towers destroyed several other nearby buildings. In all, about 2,800 people died in and near the Twin Towers. The victims included people who had been on the planes, in the Twin Towers, and on the streets below.

Survivors and **eyewitnesses** were in shock. Many of them had lost friends and relatives. "I don't know that I'm really able to describe it," New York City's mayor, Rudolph Giuliani, told reporters after the attack. "It was the most horrific scene I've ever seen in my whole life."

The South Tower collapses. The North Tower would do so in less than half an hour.

A dramatic view of the damaged section of the Pentagon. The building had been completed in 1943 during World War II.

CHAPTER SIX

"Let's Roll!"

The third hijacked airliner, American Airlines Flight 77, crashed into the Pentagon at 9:37 AM. All the passengers and crew aboard the plane were killed. Once again there was an explosion, fires, and smoke. Inside the Pentagon, another 125 people died.

Many people have wondered: why didn't the passengers fight back when the terrorists took over the airplanes? The answer is that the hijackers lied to the passengers. They assured them that nothing very bad would happen if they sat calmly. They told the passengers that they planned to land the planes safely.

However, on the fourth plane—United Airlines Flight 93—the passengers

learned the truth. After the hijackers took over Flight 93, several passengers made phone calls to their loved ones. The passengers learned that two other planes had crashed into the Twin Towers and that a third plane had hit the Pentagon. The passengers then guessed that their aircraft would also be used to destroy an important building. They quietly talked things over and decided to fight the terrorists.

On board the plane, a passenger named Tom Burnett told his wife by phone, "We're going to do something!" Shortly afterward, another man, Todd Beamer, said to his fellow passengers, "Are you guys ready? Let's roll!"

The passengers and crew fought the hijackers. As a result of the fight, the airliner crashed into a field in Pennsylvania, and everyone aboard was killed. The heroic efforts of the passengers and crew prevented the terrorists from crashing Flight 93 into the U.S. Capitol or the White House.

More Hate and Death

The victims of 9/11 at the Twin Towers included a number of Arab and Muslim people. Nearly all of the 7 million Muslim Americans in the United States condemned the 9/11 terrorist acts as wrong. Many of them donated money to help the families of 9/11 victims. Yet after the tragedy, many Muslim and Arab Americans were attacked or even killed by people who blamed *all* Muslims and Arabs for 9/11. This just added to the story of hatred and death that is 9/11.

Ten days after the attacks, workers searched through debris at the crash site near Shanksville, Pennsylvania.

The total death count from 9/11 was about three thousand people. It was the deadliest terrorist attack in history.

With the city's transportation system in chaos, thousands of people walked home across the Brooklyn Bridge.

CHAPTER SEVEN

The "War on Terrorism" So Far

Across the United States, people watched the 9/11 events unfold. They were stunned. On the evening of 9/11, President George W. Bush addressed the American people. He said:

*Today, our fellow citizens, our way of life, our very freedom came under attack in a series of deliberate and deadly terrorist acts. The victims were in airplanes or in their offices—secretaries, business men and women, military and federal workers. Moms and dads. Friends and neighbors. Thousands of lives were suddenly ended by evil, **despicable** acts of terror.*

The pictures of airplanes flying into buildings, fires burning, huge structures collapsing, have filled us with disbelief, terrible sadness, and a quiet, unyielding anger. . . . The search is underway for those who are behind these evil acts. . . .

None of us will ever forget this day, yet we go forward to defend freedom and all that is good and just in our world.

Everyone knew that the 9/11 attacks had changed the course of U.S. history. Clearly the country had to act to prevent future 9/11s from happening. Immediately the president announced what came to be called the War on Terrorism. This meant finding ways to combat terrorism at home and abroad.

For one thing, airport security became tighter. Travelers now have to put up with airport delays as security workers make sure no one brings weapons aboard airplanes. Many Americans feel that making air travel safer is worth this **inconvenience**.

Other antiterrorism decisions have been more **controversial**. The U.S. Congress passed the Patriot Act in October 2001. This law allows the government to spy on people who are thought to be linked to terrorism. In late 2002, a new government agency was created to protect the United States from terrorist attacks. It is called the U.S. Department of Homeland Security. Possibly thanks to these government actions, between 9/11/2001

Military police from the National Guard patrol Ronald Reagan Airport in Washington, D.C. The airport had been closed for nearly a month after the attacks.

and 2009 there has not been a major terrorist attack on U.S. soil.

However, this has come at a price. Many people feel that the government has seriously **violated** people's rights. For example, the Patriot Act allowed government workers to snoop on people's telephone, e-mail, and even

library records. In addition, officials have searched people's homes and offices without following the normal rules. The U.S. government has jailed many people without seeming to have the right to do so. Some of the prisoners have been mistreated. As it turned out, many of these people had no ties to terrorism anyway.

Partly as a result of 9/11, the United States also became involved in two wars in other countries. The war in Afghanistan began a month

Defending Terrorists?

Why should the United States protect the rights of accused terrorists? After all, terrorists want to kill people, right? First of all, the United States takes pride in being a fair country "with liberty and justice for all." To make these words ring true, the country must give all people a fair chance to defend themselves. Second, just because people are accused of a crime, we cannot declare that they are guilty.

after 9/11. One of the goals of the United States military was to capture Osama bin Laden, who had been living in Afghanistan. Another goal was to wipe out al-Qaeda training camps in Afghanistan. The Iraq War began in March 2003. A major reason for this conflict was that world leaders believed Iraq had dangerous **weapons of mass destruction**. Many lawmakers thought terrorists might use these terrible weapons against the United States and its allies.

A local boy stands with a group of U.S. soldiers in a province south of Kabul, Afghanistan. The troops were on a search for al-Qaeda members and weapons.

As of 2009, the Afghanistan and Iraq wars had not ended. They had cost thousands of lives without reaching their major goals. For example, Osama

Ground Zero

After the Twin Towers and nearby buildings were destroyed, the area where they stood became known as Ground Zero. Several new buildings are being put up in the Ground Zero area in New York City. One of them, the Freedom Tower, is planned to be the tallest building in North America. It will stand 1,776 feet (541 m) high. This is a meaningful number. The year 1776 was when the Declaration of Independence announced the birth of the United States.

Health Issues from 9/11

The 9/11 terrorist attacks claimed more victims months—and even years—after September 11, 2001. The collapse of the Twin Towers and the fires from the burning materials released harmful chemicals. As a result, thousands of rescue workers and people who lived and worked in the Ground Zero area became ill. They suffered from breathing problems, cancer, and other health issues. Some people have died as a result.

bin Laden had not been captured. And although al-Qaeda training camps had been bombed in Afghanistan, the country still harbored many al-Qaeda members. Furthermore, no weapons of mass destruction have been found in Iraq. Many Americans believed that these wars were not worth the thousands of lives lost.

On September 11, 2002, the first anniversary of the attacks, people visited the World Trade Center site to remember the victims.

Americans will always remember 9/11 and the people who died that day. Preventing future terrorist attacks will be one of our biggest challenges in the twenty-first century.

Glossary

ally—A friend or helper.

civilians—People who are not in the military.

controversial—Sparking disagreement or debate.

despicable—Evil and disgusting.

embassies—Offices where nations do government business in the capitals of foreign countries.

expeditions—Trips or journeys made for a specific purpose.

eyewitnesses—People who are around to see a certain event.

hijacked—Illegally took control of (as an airplane or automobile).

holy—Having special religious meaning.

hostages—People taken and held by force, often to make terrorists' enemies give in to demands.

inconvenience—Something that makes life a little bit difficult.

nuclear weapons—Very dangerous weapons whose power can ruin a city, a country, or even a continent.

prevented—Kept from happening.

seize—To take something by force.

smuggled—Sneaked into a country or building without anyone noticing.

terrorism—Large-scale, violent acts carried out by people who are not in an official army.

terrorists—People who are not in an official army and who commit violent acts against their enemies.

violated—Broke a rule or went against a right.

weapons of mass destruction—Weapons that can kill huge numbers of people.

Timeline

7:59 AM—American Airlines
Flight 11 takes off from Boston

8:14 AM—United Airlines Flight
175 takes off from Boston

8:20 AM—American Airlines Flight 77
takes off from Washington, D.C.

8:42 AM—United Airlines Flight 93
takes off from Newark, New Jersey

8:46 AM—Hijacked by terrorists, Flight
11 crashes into the North Tower of the
World Trade Center in New York City

7:59 AM   *8:14* AM   *8:20* AM   *8:42* AM   *8:46* AM

9:02 AM—Hijacked by terrorists, Flight 175 crashes into the South Tower of the World Trade Center

9:37 AM—Hijacked by terrorists, Flight 77 crashes into the Pentagon outside Washington, D.C.

9:59 AM—The South Tower of the World Trade Center falls down

10:03 AM—After passengers and crew fight the hijackers, Flight 93 crashes in a field near Shanksville, Pennsylvania

10:28 AM—The North Tower of the World Trade Center collapses

9:02 AM   9:37 AM   9:59 AM   10:03 AM   10:28 AM

Further Information

BOOKS

Englar, Mary. *September 11*. Minneapolis: Compass Point Books, 2007.

Hampton, Wilborn. *September 11, 2001: Attack on New York City*. Cambridge, MA: Candlewick Press, 2003.

Kjelle, Marylou Morano. *Helping Hands: A City and a Nation Lend Their Support at Ground Zero*. Philadelphia: Chelsea House Publishers, 2003.

Langley, Andrew. *September 11: Attack on America*. Minneapolis: Compass Point Books, 2006.

Streissguth, Thomas. *Combating the Global Terrorist Threat*. San Diego: Lucent Books, 2004.

For information and pictures of September 11 events from CNN:
http://www.cnn.com/SPECIALS/2002/america.remembers/

For a timeline of events, pictures, and other material relating to September 11 from the British Broadcasting Corporation:
http://news.bbc.co.uk/hi/english/static/in_depth/americas/2001/day_of_terror/

For coverage of the September 11 terrorist attacks from PBS:
http://www.pbs.org/newshour/bb/military/terroristattack/sept11/index.html

Bibliography

Bernstein, Richard, and the staff of the *New York Times*. *Out of the Blue: The Story of September 11, 2001, from Jihad to Ground Zero*. New York: Times Books, 2002.

Editors of *LIFE* magazine. *One Nation: America Remembers September 11, 2001*. Boston: Little, Brown, 2001.

Gilbert, Allison, and others, editors. *Covering Catastrophe: Broadcast Journalists Report September 11*. Chicago: Bonus Books, 2002.

Murphy, Dean E. *September 11: An Oral History*. New York: Doubleday, 2002.

Reporters, writers, and editors of *Der Spiegel* magazine. *Inside 9-11: What Really Happened*. New York: St. Martin's Press, 2002.

Index

Page numbers in **boldface** are illustrations.

About the Author

Dennis Fradin is the author of 150 books, some of them written with his wife, Judith Bloom Fradin. Their book for Clarion, *The Power of One: Daisy Bates and the Little Rock Nine*, was named a Golden Kite Honor Book. Another of Dennis's well-known books is *Let It Begin Here! Lexington & Concord: First Battles of the American Revolution*, published by Walker. Other recent books by the Fradins include *Jane Addams: Champion of Democracy* for Clarion and *5,000 Miles to Freedom: Ellen and William Craft's Flight from Slavery* for National Geographic Children's Books. Their current project for National Geographic is the *Witness to Disaster* series about natural disasters. *Turning Points in U.S. History* is Dennis's first series for Marshall Cavendish Benchmark. The Fradins have three grown children and five grandchildren.

4-10